THANKSGIVING
CRAFTS

BY AMY BAILEY MUEHLENHARDT
ILLUSTRATED BY NADINE TAKVORIAN

PICTURE WINDOW BOOKS
a capstone imprint

Editor: Jill Kalz
Designer: Alison Thiele
Art Director: Nathan Gassman
Production Specialist: Sarah Bennett

The illustrations in this book were created digitally and with pencil.

Picture Window Books
151 Good Counsel Drive
P.O. Box 669
Mankato, MN 56002-0669
877-845-8392
www.capstonepub.com

All books published by Picture Window Books
are manufactured with paper containing at least
10 percent post-consumer waste.

Library of Congress Cataloging-in-Publication Data
Muehlenhardt, Amy Bailey, 1974–
 Thanksgiving crafts / by Amy Bailey Muehlenhardt ;
illustrated by Nadine Takvorian.
    p. cm. — (Thanksgiving)
 Includes index.
 ISBN 978-1-4048-6282-1 (library binding)
 ISBN 978-1-4048-6721-5 (paperback)
 1. Thanksgiving decorations—Juvenile literature. 2.
Handicraft—Juvenile literature. I. Takvorian, Nadine. II. Title.
 TT900.T5M32 2011
 745.594'1—dc22
                    2010044604

Printed in the United States of America in North Mankato, Minnesota.
092010   005933CGS11

TABLE OF CONTENTS

THE THANKSGIVING *STORY*

The Pilgrims celebrated their first Thanksgiving in the fall of 1621. The harvest was plentiful that year, and the Pilgrims wanted to give thanks for their good fortune. The celebration lasted three days. The Pilgrims and their neighbors, the Wampanoag, feasted, danced, and showed off their marching and shooting skills. It was a time to get to know one another and be thankful for all they had.

This Thanksgiving, help make your family's holiday the most festive one ever. Pick a few projects from this book and get crafty. Weave a placemat. Make a Pilgrim hat. Even turn a tamborine into a turkey!

TIPS

- Gather all of your tools and supplies before starting a project.

- Have an adult help you cut cardboard and paper plates.

- Ask an adult's permission to use objects you find in the house and outdoors (pom-poms, buttons, pipe cleaners, leaves, pine cones, etc.).

- Rinse all seeds thoroughly with water before using. Spread them on newspaper to dry.

- Use freshly fallen leaves for decorating. They won't break as easily as dry ones.

- Allow drying time for your projects. The more glue you use, the longer your project's drying time will be.

GLOSSARY

angled—at a slant

brim—the edge or rim of a hat

crease—a line made by folding something

pattern—an original shape used to make more of the same shape

shuck—to remove the outer shell of a vegetable such as corn or peas

vertical—straight up and down

weave—to pass strips of material over and under one another to make something

4

PROJECT TOOLS

MARKERS

CRAYONS

PAINTBRUSHES

PENCIL

STAPLER

GLITTER GLUE

SCISSORS

MASKING TAPE

GLUE STICK

RULER

SMALL BOWLS

BAKING SHEET

GLUE

INDIAN CORN SCULPTURE

A Native-American man named Tisquantum (Squanto) taught the Pilgrims how to plant corn. He buried small fish with the seeds to make the soil better for growing.

YOU WILL NEED: a cob of corn with husk, cardboard, a pencil, scissors, glue, found objects around the house (buttons, hard candies, pom-poms, etc.)

1 Shuck the cob of corn. Save the husks and throw away the silk. Put the corn in a bag and store it in the refrigerator. You can cook it for dinner!

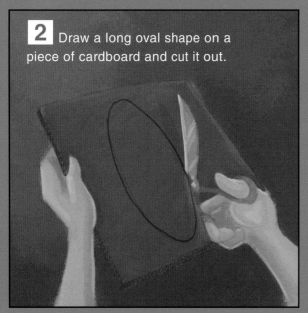

2 Draw a long oval shape on a piece of cardboard and cut it out.

3 Glue the corn husks onto the back of the cardboard. Let dry.

4 Glue your found objects onto the cardboard. Work slowly, using small pools of glue. Place the objects close together like kernels of corn.

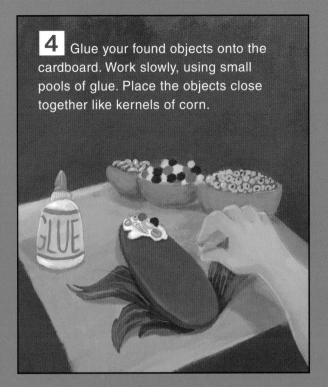

5 Continue gluing your objects onto the cardboard. Follow the curve of the cardboard.

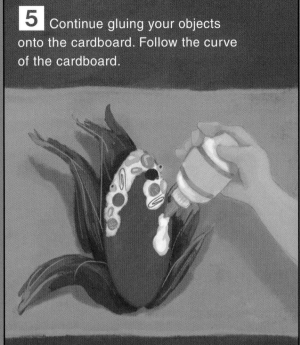

6 Let the corn sculpture dry overnight. Then display your work of art for Thanksgiving.

PILGRIM HATS

Pilgrim men and boys usually wore brown hats with wide brims, not tall black hats with buckles. Women and girls wore close-fitting cloth caps.

YOU WILL NEED: newspaper, brown paint, a paintbrush, masking tape, glue, a 12- by 15-inch (30- by 38-centimeter) piece of white construction paper, scissors, a stapler, ribbon

1 First, make the brown hat. Paint one side of two pieces of newspaper brown. Let dry.

2 Once the paint has dried, lay the two non-painted sides together. Pick up the newspaper and flatten on top of your head.

3 Ask someone to fit it to your head by wrapping a band of tape around your forehead.

4 Now that the hat has been fitted, take it off and roll the edges. Add some glue to the edges if the two pieces of paper separate.

5 Next, make the cap. Take the piece of construction paper and make a fold at the top. The fold should be long and narrow like a long rectangle.

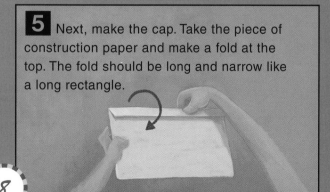

6 Fold the entire piece of paper in half so you have a center line. Open it up and lay it flat.

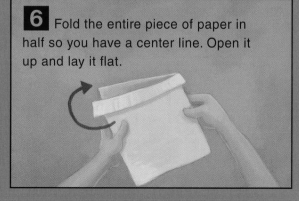

7 Make two angled cuts toward but not touching the center line. It should look like you are cutting the sides of a triangle.

8 Flip the paper so the opposite side is facing you. The folded edge should be on the bottom. Fold the bottom of the triangle toward you.

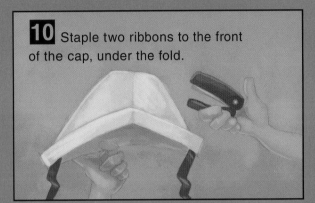

9 Fold the sides over each other. Hold together and staple through the layers.

10 Staple two ribbons to the front of the cap, under the fold.

11 Wear your hat or cap for Thanksgiving.

THANKSGIVING PLACEMATS

The Wampanoag were excellent weavers. They wove their sleeping mats using corn husks. Decorate your Thanksgiving table this year with these handmade woven placemats.

YOU WILL NEED: three pieces of construction paper in three different colors, a ruler, a pencil, scissors

1 Choose the main color for your placemat. Fold the construction paper in half.

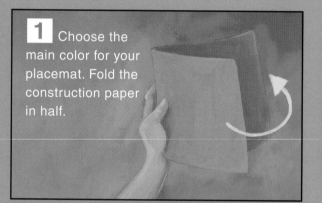

2 Create a frame. Lay a ruler on top of the folded paper. Draw lines a ruler's width from the open edges of the paper.

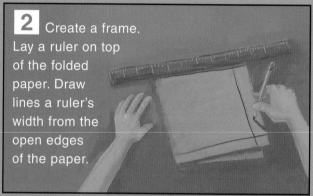

3 Holding the folded edge, cut on the vertical lines, stopping at the top line. The top line is a "no cut" line.

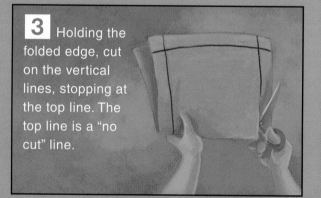

4 Cut strips between the two vertical lines. It's OK to have some strips larger than others.

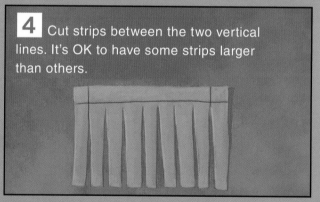

5 On the other two pieces of construction paper, draw ruler-width lines the long way. Cut along the lines to make strips.

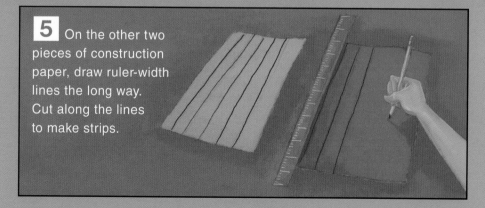

6 Open up your placemat. Line up all of the strips.

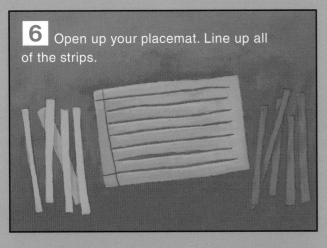

7 Time to weave! Pick up your first strip and begin pulling it over and under the cuts in the placemat.

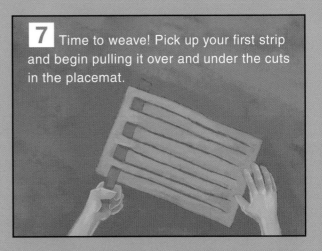

8 Now pull a strip in the other color *under and over* the cuts in the placemat.

9 Repeat steps 7 and 8 until your placemat looks like a checkerboard. Keep the strips pulled close together. You will have strips left over.

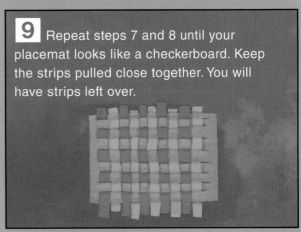

10 Flip the placemat over so you can't see the black marks. Finished!

TURKEY SNACK CUPS

Need a snack before Thanksgiving dinner? Treat your guests by filling these cups with popcorn, candy corn, dried cranberries, and other goodies.

YOU WILL NEED: construction paper (brown, orange, red, and other colors), a pencil, scissors, crayons, a paper cup, a glue stick, two black pom-poms

1 Fold part of a piece of paper. Draw a curved line on the fold. Hold the paper so the fold stays shut, and cut on the curved line.

2 Open up the cut-out shape. This is your first feather. Use it as a pattern to make four more feathers in different colors. Cut them out.

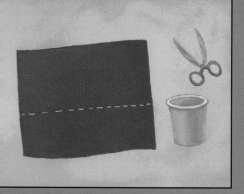

3 Use crayons to draw lines on each feather.

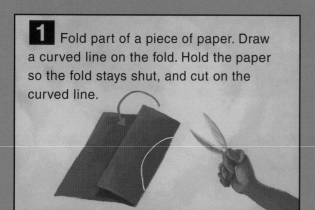

4 Place a brown piece of paper next to the cup. Cut a strip of paper about as tall as the cup and wrap it around. Glue it in place.

5 Next, glue the feathers onto the back of the cup. Be sure to fan them out.

6 To make the turkey's beak, fold part of a piece of orange paper. Draw a triangle on the fold. Cut on the lines.

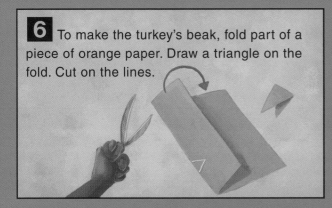

7 Glue the beak onto the cup. The backside of the beak is glued down, and the mouth is open.

8 To make the turkey's snood, cut a curvy question mark out of red paper. Glue the snood next to the beak.

9 For eyes, glue on two black pom-poms.

10 Fill the cup with snacks. Finished!

THE THANKFUL FAMILY

Thanksgiving is a time for family and friends. This year, double the fun by making your own miniature family out of clothespins. These mini family members hold everyone's reasons for being thankful. After dinner, take time to share the cards with one another.

YOU WILL NEED: construction paper, markers, a glue stick, scissors, glitter glue, clothespins (one for each member of your family)

1 Start by tracing circles for the faces of your family. Try using a glue stick cover as a pattern.

2 Now draw hair around each face. Think about each person's hair color and style. Then cut out each head.

3 Draw shirts, pants, and skirts on different colors of construction paper. Remember that each person must fit on the side of a clothespin.

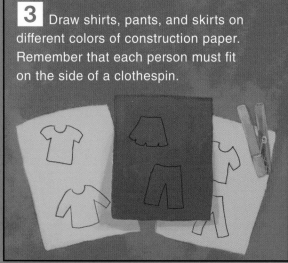

4 Cut out the clothes and add details with markers and glitter glue.

5 Lay out each person on the table before you start gluing. Add details to each face.

6 Glue the clothes onto the first clothespin. Start at the bottom, adding the head last. The clothespin should be able to stand when you are finished. Continue working on the other clothespins.

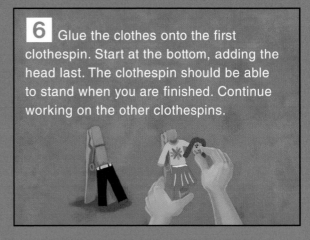

7 After all the mini family members are glued, cut cards out of the leftover construction paper.

8 Give the cards to your family members. Have them write what they are thankful for this year.

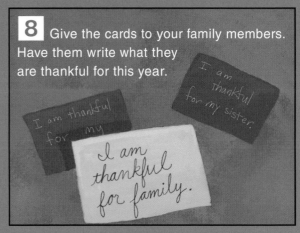

9 Clip the cards onto the clothespin people. Finished!

TURKEY POP-UP CARD

Surprise someone with a pop-up card this Thanksgiving. The turkey's beak pops right out of the center of the card!

YOU WILL NEED: two pieces of construction paper (one brown, one orange), scissors, a pencil, markers, a glue stick, crayons

1 Fold both pieces of paper in half.

2 Fold the brown paper in half again.

3 Open up the last fold made on the brown paper. You should see a crease. Starting at the fold, make a short cut on it, about an inch (2.5 cm) long.

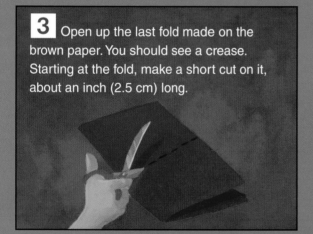

4 Lay the paper on a table with the cut toward you. Fold the corners of the cut back on both sides.

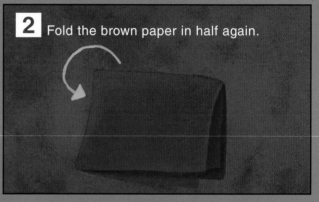

5 Flip the paper over and press the folds again. It's important to get a good crease. If the paper tears, start over.

6 Open up the paper and use your finger to pull out the bottom triangle, then the top triangle. If pulling them out doesn't work, hold the card up in the air and push the triangles into the card. You found the turkey's beak!

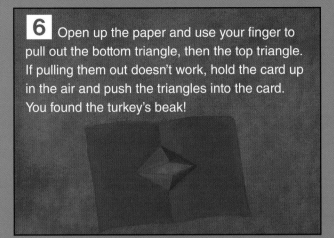

7 Close the brown paper and trace the cut on top of the orange paper. Flip the brown paper and repeat to make a diamond.

8 Draw the inside of the turkey's mouth with markers. Add a tongue and teeth.

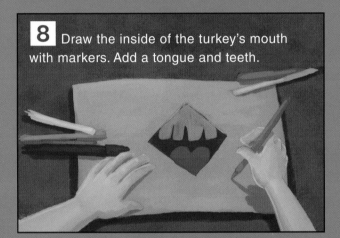

9 Open the brown paper again and glue it on top of the orange paper. Keep the beak popped out while you are gluing.

10 Use crayons and markers to draw the turkey's body, wings, legs, eyes, and feathers. Finally, close the card and design the outside of the card. Finished!

Fall Wreath

Bring the colors of fall to your front door or Thanksgiving table.

YOU WILL NEED: outdoor objects (leaves, pine cones, berries, etc.), two paper plates, scissors, a pencil, brown paint, a paintbrush, glue, pipe cleaners

1 Gather a bunch of colorful leaves and other fall treasures. Be sure to leave alone anything that is still attached to the trees or bushes. Gather objects only from the ground.

2 Cut out the center of a paper plate. Using the first plate as a pattern, trace and cut the second plate. Paint the front of one ring and the back of the other brown.

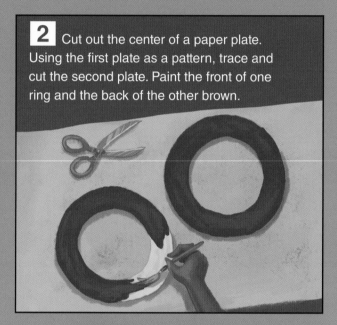

3 After the paint has dried, glue the rings, unpainted sides together. Let dry.

4 Wrap a pipe cleaner around a pine cone or other large outdoor object. Then wrap it around the ring. Use a dark color if you can, so the pipe cleaner isn't easily seen.

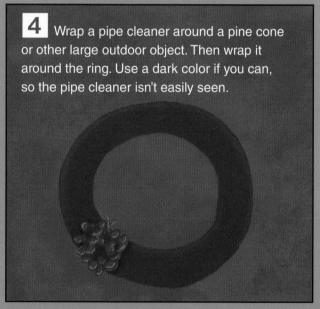

5 Tie on another pine cone. Continue to tie on or glue other outdoor objects such as pine needles or berries.

6 Next, glue on the leaves. Tuck the leaves under the pine cones and berries. Keep tucking and gluing the leaves until you can't see the brown ring.

7 Hang your wreath on the door or lay it on your Thanksgiving table. Finished!

Seed Mosaic

A mosaic is a picture made by fitting together bits of stone, glass, or other colored materials. Use seeds to create this beautiful fall mosaic.

YOU WILL NEED: seeds of different sizes and colors, newspaper, small bowls, cardboard, markers, a baking sheet, glue

1 Collect leftover seeds from a garden or scoop out seeds from gourds, pumpkins, squash ... even apples. Rinse, then dry them on newspaper.

2 Separate the seeds into bowls.

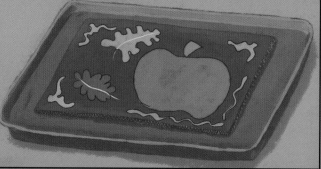

3 Use a black marker to draw a simple line picture on the cardboard. Choose something that reminds you of Thanksgiving—maybe a turkey or pumpkin. Put a curvy shape in each corner for more decoration.

4 Color your picture with markers.

5 Before you start gluing seeds, place your picture on a baking sheet. This will help keep your work area neater.

6 Squirt a little glue on one part of your drawing. It's best to start with small glue pools and work slowly and carefully.

7 Lay five or six seeds in the glue. You can use different kinds of seeds in one glue pool.

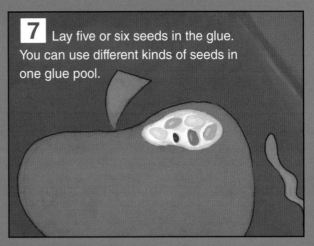

8 Keep the seeds inside the lines you drew. Turn the seeds to fit the shapes.

9 Continue working until you have filled every colored area with seeds. Let your mosaic dry overnight.

10 Lay the mosaic on the Thanksgiving table for decoration. Finished!

Turkey Tamborine

Shake! Shake! Shake! Let's make some noise this Thanksgiving with a turkey tamborine.

YOU WILL NEED: two paper plates, brown paint, a paintbrush, construction paper (brown, white, red, orange, and other colors), a pencil, scissors, glue, a stapler, dried corn kernels

1 Paint just the backs of the paper plates brown. Let dry.

2 On a brown piece of paper, draw a turkey head and wings. Cut out the parts.

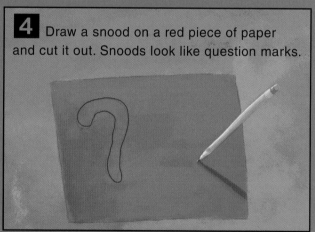

3 Draw two eyes on a white piece of paper and cut them out.

4 Draw a snood on a red piece of paper and cut it out. Snoods look like question marks.

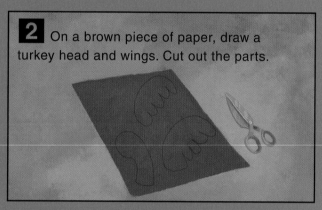

5 On an orange piece of paper, draw a beak, a feather, and two turkey legs. Cut out the parts.

6 Use the orange feather as a pattern to make more feathers of different colors. Cut them out.

7 When the plates are dry, glue the head, feathers, and legs to the white side of one plate.

8 Staple the second plate to the first, white sides together. Keep one area open so you can pour in the corn kernels.

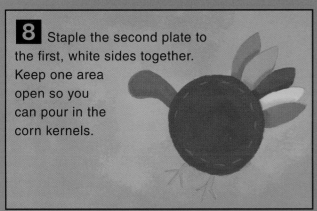

9 Glue one eye and one wing on each side of the turkey. Add the beak and snood.

10 Pour in the corn kernels and staple the last open area shut. Finished!

READ MORE

Erlbach, Arlene, and Herbert Erlbach. *Thanksgiving Day Crafts*. Fun Holiday Crafts Kids Can Do. Berkeley Heights, N.J.: Enslow Publishers, 2005.

Peppas, Lynn. *Thanksgiving*. Celebrations in My World. New York: Crabtree Pub. Company, 2009.

Sloate, Susan. *Pardon That Turkey: How Thanksgiving Became a Holiday*. New York: Grosset & Dunlap, 2010.

INTERNET SITES

FactHound offers a safe, fun way to find Internet sites related to this book. All of the sites on FactHound have been researched by our staff.

Here's all you do:

Visit *www.facthound.com*

Type in this code: 9781404862821

Check out projects, games and lots more at **www.capstonekids.com**

LOOK FOR ALL THE
BOOKS IN THE
THANKSGIVING SERIES:

Life on the Mayflower
The Pilgrims' First Thanksgiving
Thanksgiving Crafts
Thanksgiving Recipes
Thanksgiving Then and Now

INDEX

24